Let's Visit a Museum

Printed in Mexico

ISBN-13: 978-0-15-351872-0
ISBN-10: 0-15-351872-3

2 3 4 5 6 7 8 9 10   050   11 10 09 08 07 06

Harcourt
SCHOOL PUBLISHERS

Visit *The Learning Site!* www.harcourtschool.com

Let's Learn

Let's step inside a museum.
We can learn about Japan.

Let's sit in a wigwam.
We can hear about the past.
We can learn about history.

3

Let's Climb

Let's put on hard hats.
We can climb up high.

4

Let's climb in a maze.
Can we find our way out?

5

Let's Play

Let's play with blocks.
We can build things together.

Let's play in this store.
We can buy and sell food.
This museum is fun!

Think and Respond

1. What do you do in a maze?

2. How can you learn about the past?

 # Activity

Draw a picture of one thing you would do at this museum. Write a sentence about your picture.